RESET YOUR ROMANTIC GPS

Why You Steer Toward The Wrong Partners, And How To Change Direction For The Better

Marc Sholes, LCSW

When Blanche saw that … Strickland remained aloof, she … tried to bind him to herself … She pursued him with attentions … for then at least she had the illusion of holding him. … Her heart, incapable of reason…led her to believe what she wanted to be true, and…it seemed impossible to her that it should not in return awaken an equal love.

- W. Somerset Maugham,

The Moon and Sixpence

TABLE OF CONTENTS

Preface ix
    A Little About Me xi

Introduction xv

Part One: Learning About The Patterns We Operate By 1

    Attachment Style: The Big Idea 3
    What Does Attachment Style Do? 7
    Why You Want To Fix An Unhealthy Attachment 11
    Why Relationships 13
        Consequences of Unhealthy Attachments 14
    Repairing An Unhealthy Attachment Style: What's In It For Me? 19

Part Two: How Attachment Styles Work 23

    Imprinting 25
    The Big Buy 27
    The Power Of The Subconscious 29
    Types Of Attachment Styles 33
    Healthy (Secure) Attachment Style 35
    Unhealthy (Insecure) Attachment Style 39

How An Unhealthy Attachment Style Manifests In Romance 45

Compensation 51

Who To Blame: No One, Sort Of 53

Part Three: Seeking A New Home 57

Idea One: Improvement Feels Scary 59

Idea Two: Get Ready To Grieve 61

Part Four: How To Fix Your Insecure Attachment Style 65

Turn Me Right Round / Do You Remember LP's 67

The Body 69
- Exercise 69
- Sleep 74
- Diet 79

The Mind 83
- The Importance of Self-Awareness 83
- Me, Myself, and I / The Trifecta of Connectedness 84
- Meet Your Mind 88

Part Five: Choices 95

The Pepperoni Project 97

The Pull Of The Trigger 99

Cravings 101

The Big Shift 105

Take A Different Road 109

Part Six: Being With Others 113

Listening 117

Listen Up 119
Mindful Conversing 121
Never Worry Alone 123
Conclusion 125
About The Author 129

Preface

This book is for anyone who feels, sense or suspects that they are stuck in a rut, that they are not living up to their full potential, and that they are ready to make a change–in their work life, in their family relations, and most of all in their love life.

This book is a summation of what I've seen and learned in twenty-five years of being a psychotherapist in New York City.

I am not a motivational speaker, and I am not a new age guru, but if this book speaks to you as I am hoping it will, it has the potential to change your life. If I do my job in this book, you will want to commit to making this change. And though it will take discipline and a desire, I want to reassure you that making this change is not complicated.

What I want for you is a two-part deal.

Part One is for you to recognize why many–if not most, if not all–of the decisions and choices you make regarding finding your romantic partner are not your own. They're being dictated by a force that is deeply ingrained in you.

Part Two is for you to take charge of the decisions and choices you make. Because as you will see, the consequences of not doing this, of not being in charge of your own life, are devastating.

I am telling you this as a professional psychotherapist, instructor, supervisor, and teacher of psychotherapy who has seen quite a lot in my twenty-five years of practicing in New York City. I am also speaking on a personal level as an individual who has gone from someone who was not fully in charge of my own life to learning how to take charge of my choices and decisions.

In my decades of helping people in their search for happiness, stable partnerships and achieving their overall life goals, I feel that I have identified the Number One obstacle in this quest, and I am happy to say that it is a fixable condition.

It is a condition called our Attachment Style, and it can be addressed and conquered by simply becoming AWARE…aware of the deeply ingrained patterns through which we organize the world and our lives.

In this book, I will teach you about how our attachment style develops through the repetitive implicit and explicit familial interactions that we're exposed to over and over again in our early life. I'll show you how it becomes embedded in our minds.

Our attachment style becomes our internal GPS for how we navigate our world, and it continues to control our choices as adults. An area where it exerts the most influence is in romantic relationships. In this book, I'll show you how the deeply ingrained patterns that make up our attachment style obscure our ability to make conscious choices in our romantic lives. And I'll describe concrete things you can do to change it all around.

I have spent all my adult professional life–thousands of hours–counseling and observing people and couples. Anyone who knows me will tell you that I am not a carnival barker–but I can say unequivocally that if you are ready to make a change, then what I have learned will be of great help to you!

A Little About Me

The first three decades or so of my life were dominated by my preoccupation with other people's feelings, privileging other people's needs more than my own.

Though I might not have explicitly recognized that I did this, I think I had always sensed that it was part of the way I was operating. I could not remember ever not doing it and looking back I can see the devastating consequences it had on me.

In reflecting on my upbringing, it's not hard to see how my attachment style developed. My mother was a complicated woman, charismatic but also impulsive, depressive, very moody. My father was kind and caring by nature but emotionally remote. Meanwhile I was born with an empathic disposition (hence my choice of profession), and I quickly became attuned to my mother's moods, needs, and emotional longings. My job, if you will, was to regulate (balance) her emotional life and for this earned her praise, and I felt valued.

This situation in and of itself is not such a unique story. As we'll discuss later in the book, many people are subjected to the narcissistic needs of their parents, developing keen sensitivity to the moods of their caretakers, preoccupied with and privileging their parents' needs rather than their own.

But as a psychotherapist, I have been floored by the lasting power that this kind of attachment style has over one's life, as well as the severe consequences and havoc it can create along the way.

I have also learned that the only way to escape the clutches of an unhealthy attachment style is to learn about it, accept the idea of it, and then change it!

And so…

This book is for those who grew up as caretakers and accommodators, those who were required to be more attuned to their parents' needs than their parents were to theirs.

But this is not a book about blame. This book is meant to help you to gain insight into the power and the grip that your attachment style holds over you. This book is an invitation to change. Through a process of becoming aware of your attachment style, you have the opportunity to change it, and, in doing so, to create your own path.

Moving from what I call an insecure attachment style to a secure attachment style, changes your life from one where your choices are pre-determined to one where you are the one in charge, where you make choices because you want to, where you are the conductor of your own orchestra.

For those of you that this book speaks to, I cannot tell you how happy I am for you, because you are on your way to making your life much better.

Introduction

I've been practicing psychotherapy in New York City for more than a quarter of a century. In all my time of trying to help people get healthy, tidy up their worlds and straighten out their lives, I can say that, in my experience, the hands-down-number-one-no-doubt-about-it most common obstacle that people face in trying to find happiness and achieve their goals in life is this: people are unaware of the forces that draw them into their interpersonal relationships, primarily their romantic partnerships…and because of this, people waste vast amounts of precious time searching for something that they are unprepared to actually get.

I want to help you stop pairing up with the wrong romantic partners. I want to help you stop spending time and effort on the wrong relationships, and to help you get busy living the life you should be living.

Now let me be clear. Romantic problems are not the only problems my patients face. I am in no way saying that my patients (and others) who suffer from clinical conditions can fix everything by finding the right mate in life. People with clinical conditions and illnesses need to be treated in specific ways by psychological and medical professionals.

And there are, of course, millions of people whose life stories are dictated or altered by specific circumstances: injuries, illnesses, a death in the family, professional upheaval and so on. Recovery from and adjustment to these kinds of circumstances requires steps that are specific to these individuals.

What I'm talking about in this book is the much larger population of people I see, the kind of people who are walking around out there every day, getting by, even getting ahead…but never feeling truly happy or fulfilled, and never finding a real, grown up, satisfying, reciprocal relationship.

In all likelihood, if you've read this far, you are one of these people. And you most certainly know people like this.

And believe me, I know from personal experience what it's like to pursue, obsess over, hold on to, run from, maunder about, long for, and ultimately spend weeks, months and even years clinging to the wrong relationships…or trying to forget them.

It is, in a word, miserable. In a few more words, it's debilitating, frustrating, infuriating, distracting and possibly the most painful waste of our precious time on the planet.

I have learned–through experience and professional training–why some people continually go after the wrong romantic partners, how this keeps them from realizing their fullest potential in love and in life, and at what cost.

And of course, it's not only your romantic life that is negatively affected by the forces that cause you to choose the wrong partners. These forces can also wreak havoc on your work life, familial relations, and your connection to the larger world around you.

But don't despair! Because I have also learned how you can break these patterns, why it's crucial for you to do so, and the kind of upswing you can expect in your life when you get there.

The truth is that the condition you're dealing with is eminently fixable. What's more, by addressing the factors that calibrate your "romantic GPS," you will experience improvement in all areas of your life.

This book will show you how the patterns we're exposed to as very young children come to play a huge determining role in the choices we make as an adult. It will provide you with examples of people who have had experiences like yours and show you what we can learn from them. And it will provide you with basic, practical exercises and techniques you can use to bust out of the patterns that are holding you back.

I want to note here that I don't intend for this book to be a replacement for therapy. One on one therapy with a skilled therapist is a one-of-a-kind experience that can offer insight into all aspects of your specific situation.

I should also note that, while I've written this book to be as digestible as I can make it, the information it contains is backed up by thousands of hours of research and hundreds of scholarly papers. This book represents my best effort to present my own findings and those of other researchers as approachably as possible.

Because I believe that the ideas in this book can be of tremendous value to people who don't have the time, the resources, or the inclination to devote themselves to therapy or conduct full time research into human emotionality.

But make no mistake: in no way is this book a shortcut. Because there are no shortcuts when it comes to the health of our psyches.

And that's the tricky part of what we'll be discussing in this book: the fixes I advocate are not always easy. We'd all like to be George Constanza, who–in a famous episode from Seinfeld–decided one day to do everything the opposite of how he'd done things up to then…and magically his day and his life turn around for the better.

For most of us, change doesn't come quite so easily. Some of what this book has to say about your behavior, your choices and your patterns might be tough for you to accept.

But the good news is this book is not going to ask you to change yourself, just some of the things that you do. What's more, the things this book will ask you to change are not your fault.

The even better news: the key idea I want to help you understand–the one that will help you change the choices you make–is not very complicated.

Best of all: if you stick with me and put in the effort, you will see enormous positive changes in your life–*immediately*.

And that's why I wrote this book. What I want is to help people put as quick an end as possible to the patterns that hold them back. This means you! Life is too short for you to waste another minute spinning your wheels and chasing after love where you're not going to find it.

Will this book make your life 100% perfect every day of your life? Of course not. There is no such thing.

But I want to save you years of grief, frustration and wasted time. Instead of suffering through strings of bad relationships and unrequited loves, I want to help you learn much more quickly how to examine your past, partner up with the right person and start living a far more satisfying life.

The principles and ideas that I share with you in this book worked for me. Today I have a phenomenal wife and three astonishing kids. I am sure that, if you put in the work, the ideas in this book will work for you.

Your best possible life is out there waiting for you. With this book as your guide, you can start living it today.

PART ONE:

LEARNING ABOUT THE PATTERNS WE OPERATE BY

Attachment Style: The Big Idea

RACHEL* is twenty-six years old, and though she is constantly in a relationship, she has never kept any particular boyfriend around for more than nine months. Rachel tends to start a new relationship before ending the one she's currently in, meaning that most of her relationships end in fireworks, flameouts, accusations of betrayal and loud, long arguments.

Rachel is successful and reliable at work and says she's happy enough hopscotching from one boyfriend to the next and partying with her friends–though those friends report that dealing with the constant dramatics of Rachel's love life put a strain on their friendship. Rachel says she likes the idea of settling down one day–but she acknowledges that doing so would mean changing pretty much all her assumptions about how relationships work.

CARLOS is a thirty-one-year-old software engineer with a track record of serial monogamous relationships that last about three years. Carlos admits that what he likes most is the initial dance of attraction that kicks off his relationship. Carlos's interest is at its highest when he's pursuing a romantic conquest. Once the woman of the moment returns Carlos's affections, he finds that he begins to slowly lose interest. After spending eighteen months or so in a settled domestic routine, Carlos then spends anywhere from six to twelve months figuring out how to extricate himself from his situation without hurting his partner too much.

After all, he's not out to inflict pain on his partner–but he does want to be free to begin the chase all over again.

As he gets older, Carlos finds that the cycle of pursue-acquire-domesticate-reject doesn't deliver quite the thrill that it used to…but he's content to keep it up until his system unearths the one person who can not only capture his interest but maintain it into the future.

JAMES is forty-seven. He's a successful surgeon who has never been married. He has had a string of long-term relationships–but eventually all his partners moved on, because James would never commit to marrying them, or even provide them assurance that he was in the relationship for the long haul. James has strong feelings for the women he has had relationships with, and in fact he stays in touch with many of his past partners. Still, he would never "go all in" with them for good, because in the back of his mind he always held out the possibility that someone better might come along–and he didn't want to miss that opportunity.

RESET YOUR ROMANTIC GPS

A few years ago, James's latest relationship was nearing its end–but then his partner became pregnant, and she decided to keep the baby. So, James decided to give the relationship one more try. He moved in with his partner; they are living together and raising their daughter as a committed couple. Still, despite his partner's stated desire, James refuses to marry her. When the subject comes up, he tells her that maybe they can do it one day, but since things are fairly stable now, he sees no reason why they need a piece of paper to formalize their arrangement.

(*All names in this book have been changed.)

* * *

Do you know someone like one of the people I've just described?

Are you yourself like one of the people I've just described? Or at least a close facsimile?

If you're answer to either question is yes (and I'd bet a slice of pizza that it is), then welcome to the club.

And actually, the truth is that you have belonged to this club your whole life. As have Rachel and Carlos and James, and billions of other people. As different as you all are, you all have one thing in common that qualifies you for instant membership in the club.

That qualification is this: you have all had a childhood.

And the fact that you (and I, and everyone else on this planet) had a childhood means that you (and I, and everyone else on this planet) also developed a certain characteristic common to all of us.

This characteristic is called your ATTACHMENT STYLE. Very briefly, your attachment style is your psyche's reaction to the emotional environment in which you were brought up. It is what provides you with your sense of what "normal" is when it comes to emotional relationships.

Attachment styles develop in roughly the first eighteen months of life. They are a product of the family and relationship experiences you have during that most impressionable time. And though they develop early, attachment styles play a dominant role in the lives in the majority of adults.

After years of working in the field of psychotherapy, I am still truly humbled by the power that our initial familial relationships have in the shaping of our brains and of our experience. We are born into a world of relationships, healthy or unhealthy, and we organize ourselves around the patterns that we experience over and over in those early months.

Many want to believe that the way we conduct ourselves as adults is more complicated than that, but the truth is that much of our behavior is patterned on what we learn before we can write our name. It's that simple.

Teaching you about the power that your attachment style has over your life–and why it's so important to take that power back–is what this book is all about.

What Does Attachment Style Do?

While every person is different, and everyone's journey through life is his or hers alone, we do undergo common experiences as we develop, grow and mature.

Attachment style is one of the earliest, most fundamental and most formative of these experiences.

Attachment style is a broad, deep, and fascinating area of human psychology–but for now, let's start with the basic idea that is at the heart of this book.

Simply put, your attachment style develops during your first eighteen months (or so) of life. It is based on your experience of yourself, your family, and the world at that tender age. And it then determines what feels emotionally and psychologically normal to you from then on. Your attachment style establishes your emotional "home," the kind of emotional "place" that feels familiar and safe to you– even if that place is not so nice.

That's it. This idea–that our attachment style, our idea of "normal," is the all-powerful dictator of our emotional lives– is going to drive the rest of this book.

Of course, there's a little more to it than that; the rest of this book isn't just filled with pastry recipes.

But for now, as a way of letting the idea of attachment style sink in, I want you to try something.

Close your eyes (not right now; wait till you finish reading this section!) and imagine that I just told you that there is this thing that you had never heard of, and that this thing is called an air conditioner.

Imagine that I went on to say that an air conditioner is a complicated machine, but that, in essence, it does a very specific, self-contained job. An air conditioner is a machine that makes the air cool.

I haven't told you anything about how an air conditioner works, about what can go wrong with an air conditioner, or about how to fix an air conditioner. But already you know the most fundamental thing about it. An air conditioner is an air-cooling machine. You set the dial, turn it on, and cool air comes out. Think about that.

Now do the same thing with the idea of attachment style. For the moment, don't worry about how an attachment style works, where it comes from, what happens when it goes wrong, how to fix it and all the rest of it. For now, simply think about this basic idea: that–in much the same way as an air conditioner is an air-cooling machine, a person's attachment style works like an emotional pattern-setting "machine." You set it in early childhood, turn it on, and the emotional choices you make for the rest of your life come out.

Let that sink in. Try to accept this idea: you carry within you an emotional-choice-making machine whose knobs were set very, very early in your life.

It's not an easy idea to swallow. Most adults like to think that they're in control of their lives. The thought that experiences you had before you could even walk are dictating the emotional moves you make today ... that's a pretty big meatball.

What's more, you don't know how this emotional-choice-making machine works. You don't know what can happen when it's not running right. And you don't know how to fix it.

But don't worry. We're going to spend the rest of this book learning how to change all that, together.

Why You Want To Fix An Unhealthy Attachment

I hope you had an amazing childhood, during which you developed a 100% healthy (secure) attachment style. I hope your parents were strong, loving, committed to one another, and were able to lavish their love and attention and support on you in a way that was not overbearing but instead gave you the confidence and the wings to soar off in pursuit of your dreams.

Some people were blessed to have childhoods like this. It's impossible to say how many, but drawing on my professional expertise, I'd put that number at about five…or I'd at least say that sometimes the number feels that low.

All kidding aside, the truth is that there are people out there who had the kinds of psychologically bulletproof upbringings that set them up to succeed in life without the small, medium, or large emotional issues that the rest of us commonly experience.

If you are one of those people: congratulations.

For the rest of us, the fact is that attachment style is a phenomenon we all must deal with in one way another. We are all somewhere on a spectrum of attachment style "disorders" that ranges from Mildly Influential to Hugely Debilitating.

Like it or not, our attachment styles are a fact of our lives. And since you only go around once, that means there is no time to waste! So, let's get to work on understanding the way our attachment style influences our decisions in life…and then set about changing that arrangement.

Why Relationships

Attachment Style influences everything: our careers, our dealings with family members, our outlook on life, even our physical health.

So why does this book focus so heavily on romantic relationships? Because we humans are creatures of relationships. A lasting, loving relationship with another person might not be for everybody–but for 99% of humanity, an intimate relationship with another person is the most central factor in their adult lives.

What's more, the inability to truly connect with an intimate partner is the most common and easy to understand effect of an unhealthy (or "insecure") attachment style. The emotional and psychological wrinkles that appear as people pursue relationships offer very concrete illustrations of the many ways that our attachment styles affect us.

And finally–and here's the good news–a person's inability to form real intimate relationships because of an unhealthy attachment style turns out to be eminently fixable. When my patients begin to truly understand the power that attachment style has over their relationships, they see immediate dividends. They go from hopeless to hopeful, from anxious to confident–and they finally start finding the *right* types of people attractive.

And as people "fix" their unhealthy attachment styles and begin enjoying solid, healthy, supportive, and loving relationships, they find that there is a profound and positive spillover effect in other areas of their lives.

It is my hope is that, by teaching you about attachment styles and improving your ability to maintain a great relationship, the rest of your life will blossom as well.

Consequences of Unhealthy Attachments

Before we get into the mechanics of how attachment styles work, I want to start with an overview of some of the consequences of an unhealthy attachment style, so you can understand why you should be concerned with attachment style in the first place.

Let's begin by using the time-honored and always effective laundry list format. Ready?

A Sampler of the Life Effects of Unhealthy Attachment Styles:

- Passive aggressive behavior
- Procrastination
- Depression
- Anxiety
- Alcohol abuse
- Substance abuse
- Feeling of emptiness
- Shame
- Powerlessness
- Controlling behaviors
- Passively waiting for things to change

- General, gnawing unhappiness

Yeesh. Not a very savory menu of options, I think you'd agree.

Now let's take a look at how some of these ripple effects might typically play out in the lives of people with unhealthy attachment styles.

Sara's boyfriend Tom has just broken up with her, and all she thinks about is how to get him back. She is overwhelmed with anxiety, and the only thing that helps her feel marginally better is contact with Tom. Sara has become consumed with the thought "had she just done something differently, Tom would have stayed with her".

Tom shares many characteristics with Sara's aloof and rejecting father. When Tom broke up with Sara, he blamed her for ruining the relationship with her neediness and insecurity–using many of the same words that Sara's father used when arguing with Sara's mother.

Over the course of their relationship, all Sara wanted was to make Tom happy; she was self-sacrificing and extremely attuned and sensitive to him. But he always focused on her faults–and when he did so, Sara would feel rejected and become self-doubting. Sara would also become angry, but she hid her anger, fearing that it might push Tom away.

Now Sara doubts herself and questions her own sense of reality. She knows Tom didn't treat her particularly well, but she wonders if that might be her fault. Maybe Tom is a better person than Sara gives him credit for, she thinks maybe the hitches in their relationship were her fault. She goes on to wonder whether her entire perspective on life is skewed; maybe her own needs are unreasonable.

Sara is isolated and depressed. She reports that she does not like the kind of person Tom is, and she can tick off a host of reasons why he did not make a good partner. Still, she can't let go of him, and she's obsessed with getting him to see her differently than he currently does.

At forty, ERIC still cannot commit to his girlfriend, even though he wants to, and even though everyone else in his circle is already married with children. He thinks he loves his girlfriend, and he wants to make her happy, but he can't seem to feel "that thing" that would get him over the hump.

Eric is a very agreeable and helpful guy but can't see the benefit of marriage. He fears he will get suffocated and "go numb" if he commits; it has happened to him in the past, and even now he can sense the same feeling creeping into his current relationship. He holds out hope that someday someone else will come along who will make him feel different. For Eric, time seems to be standing still.

ALAN, twenty-six, does not understand why things seem to be so easy for other people. He is as smart as his successful friends. But somehow, they seem to be able to focus and learn and accomplish and get ahead in life, while Alan feels like he can't express his creativity. He is too scared to go out on a limb and stay out there.

Alan often finishes his days with the feeling that he hasn't accomplished what he wanted to. He spends a lot of his time distracted, unable to focus on his work, watching pornography, craving unhealthy "comfort" foods, and dreaming of the things he wishes could be. There are many ways he soothes himself, but they are all secret–and though he dreams of being more successful in business and in his relationships, he doesn't know how he would let go his self-regulating ways and commit to living a life that demands him to be more present. Alan does not understand any other way to make himself feel better, and he doesn't understand how relationships could be nourishing rather than just a source of disappointment.

All of these adults are suffering from the consequences of an attachment style they developed *before they could even read.*

And as you can see, the effects of an unhealthy attachment style are–to use a clinical term–"no fun."

So, let's change the mood.

Repairing An Unhealthy Attachment Style: What's In It For Me?

In a word: Everything!

When you learn how to break the hold that your unhealthy attachment style has on you, you are no longer its slave. You're free!

For the first time, you begin to have real choices–*your* choices. And with choices comes control…empowerment…the feeling of being in charge of your own life for a change!

As you let go of your old attachment needs, the first relationship that will improve is the *relationship you have with yourself.* Old feelings like boredom, anxiety and self-loathing will slip away. Instead, you will experience a new version of yourself that you will like a whole lot better.

Soon enough you will begin to build *self*–as if you were finally exercising a long-disused muscle. And sure, it can be a little tough. There's resistance, and soreness and stiffness. But just like a productive workout, building yourself can feel good even when it hurts.

Your other relationships will also improve–relations with colleagues, friends and family will take off. You'll find you have less time and energy for the unhealthy relationships in your life–say with friends who depend on you overextending yourself on their behalf–but all the other ones will begin to glow more brightly.

And you will begin to develop a much stronger and more vital sense of well-being. You'll be more energetic, more enthusiastic, and ultimately–dare to dream here.

And you'll make those who are closest to you happy too!

It's a win-win-win.

And the thing is, it's up to you: you can keep doing the same things you've always been doing and hope for a different result. Or you can take a little time to learn about how attachment styles operate and consider whether the one that makes you tick might benefit from a reset.

The incentives are plain enough. If you'd like to get in on 'em, then let's pop the hood and take a look at what really makes attachment styles run.

PART TWO:

HOW ATTACHMENT STYLES WORK

This is the part of the book where I go into detail about how all the big emotional decisions you are making as an adult stem from and are governed by the emotional experience you had with your parents and your world in the first eighteen months of your life.

Let me go on to say: I KNOW that the idea that your early experience in life have an outsized influence on your present-day existence is a lot to swallow, but it is true.

And if you think that's crazy, then brace yourself–because there are even more seemingly outlandish claims to come.

Even so, by the end of this section, my goal is to have you come around to a few simple ideas.

1. The emotional patterns we're exposed to very early in life set the table for the emotional decisions we make as adults
2. This is true for everyone, kings, paupers, trumpet players, prima ballerinas, accountants, and sous chefs.
3. It's not your fault, and
4. Once you understand and accept this idea, you can change your day-to-day reality for the better.

Ready? Great. Let's start with the most basic of the basics, the idea of Imprinting.

Imprinting

Avid watchers of nature shows (or actual nature) will be familiar with the idea that many newborn animals have the ability to instantly memorize their mother's physical appearance the moment they're born.

Baby zebras instantly memorize their mom's unique stripe pattern. Greylag geese identify the first moving stimulus they see as their mother and follow it around incessantly. There are numerous other examples among birds and mammals–creatures with strong parent-offspring relationships.

Imprinting is a survival instinct, ensuring (as much as possible) that a youngster won't get separated from his or her mother.

And the fact is that it's not only birds and zebras that imprint. People do it too. But whereas other animals imprint according to the physical characteristics of their parents, humans imprint according to their parents' *emotional and relational* characteristics.

And while other animals do it instantly, or within the first few hours of their lives, with people, the process takes a little longer. Human emotional imprinting develops over the course of a child's first eighteen months of life.

Animal imprinting serves the purpose of "telling" a newborn goose or zebra what safety and security and home look like. That is, a zebra's mom represents the idea of safety and security and home to that young zebra–and imprinting tells that zebra "find this particular visual pattern–the pattern of your mom–and you will be safe."

And here's the crucial element of the idea of attachment styles. While animal imprinting "tells" baby animals what safety and security and home *look* like, imprinting in humans tells young children what safety and security and home *feel* like. So, while animal imprinting tells newborns to seek out a particular and familiar visual pattern in order to be safe, human emotional imprinting tells us to seek out a particular and familiar *emotional pattern* in order to feel safe.

Because humans are such emotional creatures, our imprinting–our sense of safety, and familiarity, and a *home*– is based on emotion more than on physical characteristics.

The Big Buy

And here we come to the thought that my patients–and most others I speak with about attachment styles–have the most difficulty swallowing. But it's the one that you must accept if you are going to change your attachment style and swing your choices around from negative to positive on the Life-O-Meter.

The idea is this: children who imprint in negative, chaotic, unsupportive, and even toxic emotional environments will seek out similarly negative environments in their adult relationships–*even if those relationships make them miserable*–precisely because the negativity, the chaos, the toxicity *feel like home. They feel familiar. THEY MAKE US FEEL SAFE. Or the closest thing to safety that we knew.*

Yes. If we are raised in "messy" (if you'll allow the term) circumstances, then messy feels normal. It feels familiar. It is what we imprint on. And it sets the knobs on our emotional-choice-making machine–our attachment style. And it is what we return to in order to feel safe and at home.

For many, this is a tough idea to accept. Because the opposite is what seems obvious: if our upbringings were "miserable," wouldn't we do everything in our power to run the other way.

And the answer is: NO. Because that is not how people work.

Instead, this is how we work.

The Power Of The Subconscious

When I was a kid, I went to a stage hypnotist show with a friend of mine, Dave, and his parents. It was one of those performances where the hypnotist pulls people out of the audience, instantly puts them to "sleep" and then gives them all these crazy instructions ("You're a chicken! Now act like a chicken!") which they then proceed to carry out onstage.

Afterwards, we went out to a noisy, crowded restaurant, and Dave's mom asked how it was possible for the hypnotist to do what he did. Dave's dad–a psychiatrist who has some experience with hypnosis–offered to show her.

So right there, Dave's dad put his mom under hypnosis (they have a very cool, fun-loving relationship). And when she was under, Dave's dad gave his wife this set of instructions. He told her that when he brought her out of hypnosis, she would feel great. He also told her that when he took a sip of his beer, she would remove her necklace and put it in her purse.

Dave's dad then brought his mom out of hypnosis. She seemed completely fine. Then, after a minute or two, Dave's dad took a very conspicuous sip of his beer. Dave's mom put her hand up to her neck … but then hesitated. A look of confusion came over her.

Dave's dad said, "What's up?" and he took another conspicuous sip of his beer. Dave's mom said "Nothing." Then she said, "I have to do something with my necklace."

Dave's dad said "Huh? What do you mean?"

Dave's mom said: "I don't know. I have to put it in here." She pointed to her purse.

Dave's dad: "How come?"

Dave's mom: "It's important."

Dave's dad: "How could that be important?"

Dave's mom could come up with no rational reason why she had to put her necklace in her purse–but nonetheless she felt compelled to do it. To the point where she finally said: "I don't know, but I have to do it. I, ummmm, don't want to get food on it."

She removed her necklace and put it in her purse. She looked visibly relieved, but also puzzled.

Then, after a moment, she looked at Dave's dad. "Did you give me a post-hypnotic suggestion?" she asked.

Dave's dad looked pleased. "Yes, I did," he said.

Dave's dad went on to explain that hypnosis accesses the subconscious mind: the layer of our minds that operates beneath the level of the thinking we do when we're awake and conscious. It is also the place in our minds where our deeply ingrained organizing patterns–our attachment styles–reside.

Doing math, writing a letter, meeting friends for lunch, delivering a speech–these are handled by our conscious minds.

The subconscious mind deals more fundamentally with emotions. But it is extremely powerful, it is always operating just beneath the surface of our conscious thoughts, and it exerts a huge influence on our conscious lives.

And that's why Dave's mom *had* to put her necklace in her purse. Consciously, she could come up with no good reason why she needed to do so. But the need to do it had been planted in her subconscious–and the subconscious mind is so powerful, that Dave's mom went ahead and did it.

And not only did she do it, she then went on to make up a reason why she needed to do it–to keep from spilling soup on it.

And this is the final point: When our subconscious minds make us do something completely irrational (like removing a necklace for no reason), our conscious minds are compelled to come up with a reason–also known as a "rationalization"–for why we're doing it.

Our rational mind does this because people don't like to feel like they are not in conscious control of the things they do. So, we make up reasons for the things our subconscious makes us do so that we can feel as if we are doing them by choice…and not because some unconscious force that we don't understand is compelling us to do so.

The struggle for power between the conscious and the subconscious is always going on within all of us. The more we become aware of what is taking place within us at a subconscious level, the more we can bring these two sides of our consciousness into harmony–and exert more conscious control over the choices we make.

The idea of that the subconscious exerts a huge influence on our conscious lives is crucial to recognizing the power that our attachment style has over our romantic choices.

Because, as I said, our attachment style develops very early on–in the first eighteen months of life, before our consciousness truly begins to develop. Thus, our attachment style is imprinted on the level of our subconscious mind.

And just as a post-hypnotic suggestion implanted in our subconscious mind can make us do things that make no rational sense–such as removing our necklace in a crowded restaurant for no good reason–so the attachment style that implanted (developed) in our subconscious during our earliest stages of development comes to determine the choices we make as adults.

Types Of Attachment Styles

The writer Kurt Vonnegut once used the image of a stack of cannon balls on a courthouse lawn to illustrate the idea of pattern setting. It went like this:

Think of a stack of cannon balls on a courthouse lawn. The first layer of the stack determines the pattern for the rest of the stack. A triangular first layer dictates a pyramid. A circular first layer dictates a cone. And so on...

The same is true of our earliest relationships. After years of working in the field of psychotherapy, I am still humbled every day by the power that our initial familial relationships have in the shaping of all the relationships we have for the rest of our lives. Humans are born into a world of relationships, and we organize ourselves around the patterns that we are exposed to in early childhood.

Like a stack of cannon balls on a courthouse lawn, those first relationships dictate the kinds of relationships we go on to seek out for the rest of our lives.

It sounds simple–and many want to believe that the relationship issues that many of us face are more complicated than that–but the truth is that we (and our problems) are really that basic.

So basic, in fact, that I can break attachment styles into two broad categories: HEALTHY and UNHEALTHY (SECURE AND INSECURE ATTACHMENT STYLES). Let's get to know 'em.

Healthy (Secure) Attachment Style

...or what we clinicians call a "secure" attachment. It starts with parents who are attuned to the needs of a child. These parents organize a child's emotional, social, and physical world in such a way that, beginning in infancy, the child is raised with the reasonable expectation that her needs will be met by her parents or other responsible adults.

Children who experience this "attuned" parenting over the course of thousands of "relationship (relational) moments" (from diaper changes to eye contact during mealtime to reading aloud and so on) are generally quick to develop a sense of safety in the world, a sense that the rest of the world will meet them, will like them and support them.

And when these individuals meet with disappointment–as they inevitably will–they don't completely fall to pieces. Their secure attachment style has provided them with a base of confidence and stability that will help see them through the tough times with hope and resiliency.

Individuals with secure attachment styles have a greater ability to delay gratification in pursuit of deeper satisfaction. Rather than panicking at the first sign of trouble, these individuals tend to experience life events deeply and thoughtfully, and they make life choices that reflect those qualities.

Raising children with a secure attachment style provides them with an internal safety net that provides reassurance as they move through life. A secure attachment style is truly the gift that keeps on giving.

Qualities of Secure Attachment Parenting

- Parents who can see a child's perspective on life
- Parents who are collaborative
- Parents who are self-reflective and self-aware
- Parents who are capable of empathy–i.e., the ability to put themselves in the other's shoes.

Descriptions of the Secure Attachment Parents

- "My parents valued relationships"
- "They were attentive and supportive"
- "They repaired ruptures when they happened and did not hold grudges."
- "My parents like closeness, they were physically demonstrative and hugged us."
- "Our household was not an overly anxious one."

Qualities of a Secure Attached Person

- I am resilient
- I get along with people
- I can leave you if you are not good for me
- I like complexity

RESET YOUR ROMANTIC GPS

- I do not fear a challenge
- I do not experience loss as abandonment
- I am not afraid of being engulfed

Unhealthy (Insecure) Attachment Style

And now for the other side of the attachment coin: insecure attachment parenting.

Before we get into this aspect of attachment styles, I want to say a word on behalf of all the parents out there, and it is this: in the vast majority of cases, parents really do want what's best for their kids. They work hard to be good parents. They mean well. They do the best they can.

But parents are people, and they are flawed, and you don't have to be a monster to make mistakes. So, while there is a reason why Child Services agencies do exist, most parents are genuinely trying to be the best parents they can be.

But despite their best intentions, many parents do create the kind of conditions that lead to the development of an insecure attachment style.

Insecure attachment parenting takes place in an environment where the parents' emotional and physical attunement to their child is inadequate, non-existent, or downright toxic.

Parents in these environments are only occasionally available to their children (in both the emotional and literal senses), or ignore their children, or mistreat them, or even emotionally or physically abuse them.

In these environments, it is the child who is required to accommodate in order to meet a parent's needs–rather than the other way around.

These children learn to doubt and blame *themselves* for their relational and emotional "dislocation"–that is, they recognize that something is off, but rather than pointing the finger at a parent, the child with an insecure attachment style will blame himself for the problem. The child does this not only because it feels safer, but also because it gives him a sense of control over things.

"If I can just get it right, if I can just change my behavior in the right way," the thinking goes, "then my parent's love will be forthcoming."

This thought pattern puts the responsibility on the child and puts the status of his relationship with his parent in his hands.

Of course, the one who should be responsible for the relationship is the adult. But instead, the child is left to work things out on his own. He internalizes a constant backbeat of anxiety and danger. He learns not to value his own inner needs; indeed, he becomes ashamed of them. He becomes hyper-attuned to the Other–to the grownups around him. The child's main motivation now is *not* to explore the world with curiosity and confidence, but to ward off danger, to avoid loneliness, and to search for the kind of connection that will make up for the one he lacks with the caretakers who are charged with caring for him.

And this is where the idea of imprinting really comes into play. Because to individuals with insecure attachments, their "inner home" is not one of peace and security and harmony. Instead, their inner home is a place characterized by disconnection, insecurity, and disharmony.

"Home" feels like chaos and dysregulation. And it is infused with feelings of abandonment and self-doubt.

Even worse: experiences that should feel emotionally healthy and regulating–like a stable relationship with a trusted and trusting partner–feel unfamiliar and threatening to the insecurely attached person. They feel almost like a state of homelessness because this person only recognizes home as a state of disconnection and dysregulation. And happiness is something that happens only in some strange, foreign place.

The consequences of this phenomenon can be tragic if they are not changed. The child never gets her authentic needs met: the anxiety of her existential aloneness in never validated or understood, comforted, or soothed. So, in order to feel tethered to the world, the child becomes hyper attuned to the needs of others. She becomes a "pleaser," avoiding conflict and doubting herself, because early in her development she learned that if she tried to exert her own authentic needs, she would fail to connect to her caretakers.

What's more, because this person has expended so much of her energy and assertiveness and emotional life in an effort to be hyper-attuned to her parents–and then others–that she has never fully explored her own self. Her thrust for life, her psychic energy and her intrinsic assertiveness have been depleted on her being hyper-attuned to her parents needs and so the vast majority of her potential remains untapped.

At this point in life, the only arsenal that this child/adult possess in their relationship to their world is their skill at attempting to ward off overwhelming feelings of aloneness and anxiety managed through the act of accommodation.

And so, for the insecurely attached person, longing is the dominant state of being. It is a state, in which the person experiences the need to return home continuously.

According to the Merriam-Webster dictionary, "longing" is "a strong persistent yearning or desire, especially one that cannot be fulfilled."

Longing of this sort, can lead to a lifetime of ruminating, about what you wish could work, what in your heart you believe should work. If only they could understand me; if only I had another chance, if only I could get it right! The insecurely attached person is hopelessly drawn to the void of the unattainable.

And so, for the insecurely attached person, longing is what "home" feels like and the lack of longing; contentment-feels unfamiliar, scary, and threatening.

The insecurely attached person is repeatedly and irresistibly drawn to the unavailable–because it feels normal to them. Because it is what connectedness feels like for them. Because it feels like home.

Qualities of Insecure Attachment Parenting

- Parents valued extreme independence
- Parents take care of themselves first
- "It's a competitive world"
- Neediness brings on contempt
- Vulnerability is a weakness

Qualities of an Insecure Attached Person

- I am clingy
- I had to regulate at least one parent
- I was rewarded and valued for taking care of one or both of my parents
- I am all about relationships and closeness
- I put others' needs above my own
- I like to "fix people" and I am drawn to people who cannot be fixed
- If I can fix you, I begin to lose interest
- I need to be needed
- I am passive aggressive because I am afraid to assert my needs
- I am critical of others
- I have secrets
- I have ways of regulating myself that you will never know
- I don't share
- I am self-righteous
- I like perfection
- I have shame about my needs
- If you knew me, you would not like me
- I have a temper when cornered

And so… you'd think that the rational thing for someone from a detached or dysfunctional or toxic upbringing would be to run from similar circumstances as an adult. But as we've just seen, a huge part of us–the one that makes us put our necklace in our purse when there's no good reason to do so–exerts enormous influence over the decisions we make and actions we take.

Because it very desperately wants to recreate the conditions it was raised in, our subconscious causes us to make the irrational choice of seeking out and reproducing those conditions in our lives, over and over again.

How An Unhealthy Attachment Style Manifests In Romance

The power of our subconscious to make us put that necklace in our purse, to cause us to act according to its will even if the actions it wants us to take are completely irrational...that power manifests itself in most areas of our lives: work, family relations–even our political leanings according to some studies.

But this book is primarily about your love life, so let's take a look at how our status as "home-seeking missiles" affects our decisions in *les affaires de l'amour* (I'm taking an online French course).

Okay. Sandra...and Jeff...and Stu and Marta and Constance and George–and hundreds of millions of others–were raised in emotionally erratic circumstances that instilled in them a preoccupation with the needs of OTHERS...

So, to achieve a sense of stability and security in their own lives, they learned even in their first few months to forgo their own needs. Which means they literally became out of touch with themselves.

I'll say that more loudly: people with an insecure attachment style that has caused them to place the needs of others before their own needs quite literally do not know themselves.

Now I'll say it more personally: Since feeling loved for being your authentic self is NOT an experience that you identified with as a youngster, and since you were not trained to prioritize or connect with your authentic needs, then, as a home-seeking missile, you are NOT going to be attracted to someone who is capable of truly loving *you*, of honoring your actual self. Because that would feel completely foreign and un-home-like to your subconscious.

Even worse, you are not going to be attracted to someone who wants to put a priority on your needs. Worse still–you are not going to be attracted to someone who wants to connect with the real you–since the real you is the one thing that you have been trained since birth to bury.

Remember: if your earliest needs were not valued, respected, and responded to in ways that they truly deserved, then your sense of self-worth has come from your ability to read and respond to the others in your life, to privilege and take care of their needs.

So, if you're not going to go after someone who really wants a crack at your true inner self, then who are you going to go for?

Well, life is complicated and not everyone is the same all the time–but the Vegas odds makers would say that ninety-nine times out of a hundred, you're going to go for someone who is selfish, someone who likes their needs to be in the foreground, someone who is aloof, someone who is ambivalent about commitment, someone who is depressed–or that magical object of love who combines some or all of these qualities.

RESET YOUR ROMANTIC GPS

Tragically, for the insecurely attached person, that feeling of *chemistry* is often associated with a person or situation that strongly resembles their original faulty attachments and what ultimately feels familiar is the body's recognition that they are with someone who resembles their original home.

What happens when you meet this guy or gal?

First, your radar starts to go "Bloop! Bloop! Bloop!" Whoa! A target on the scope! Your pupils dilate, and your nervous system sparks up, recognizing that sense of familiarity and hopefulness.

"Home!" your nervous system says.

You want to go there. You want to go home. And what do you hope to gain by going home?

One possibility is that, if you can connect with this person, if you can win them over, if you can charm, cajole, or coerce them into responding to you, then you can repair the old traumas you suffered back in your infancy and childhood. Another possibility is that you recognize this person as the kind of individual you know how to "connect with." As embodied by this person, home is calling–and home is the big draw for those with insecure attachment styles.

In the first case, the feeling is that if you can make this relationship work, it will make up for the one from your childhood that didn't work. In the second case, the feeling is the satisfaction that comes from being with someone you really "know how to be with."

47

And so, you tell yourself: "What if my ability to read this person, my sensitivity to this person's needs, could catch their eye, could draw them in. And this time, unlike my parents and all my previous relationships, this person will finally see how valuable I can be. I will surrender myself and accommodate this person and tend to their needs *in a way that nobody ever tended to my own.*"

And so–you charge off in pursuit of this person. You feel excited. The thrill of the chase! It's the same kind of jolt an addict gets when he's preparing to indulge in his drug of choice.

And for a moment, when you first hook up with this person, you feel a burst of chemistry, and you experience a sense of wholeness…that rush of conquest and achievement, and maybe even a sense of togetherness with this person…

Except it's not real in the sense that you are the one making the decisions. The driver of this choice is your attachment style. Your *sirens* are calling, and you are reflexively responding. You are not likely making a conscious choice.

And so, what you initially experience as a moment of powerful togetherness turns out to be fleeting. It requires the subordination of your *self*–because that's how you know how to connect. And that, in all likelihood is what the other person expects in a partner. (And I'll have more to say about these "other people" elsewhere–because they are a subject of their own.)

So now, instead of your moment of togetherness leading to continued intimacy, you instead become concerned–scared, even–that the closeness won't last. So, you start focusing your energy on preserving that closeness, on not losing the feeling you've managed to conjure up. And suddenly, you're not in a relationship with a person, you're in a relationship with a feeling. That feeling of, if I just get this right, then the love and security I have always wanted will be in reach. And it's a relationship based on fear–the fear of losing that feeling and the relationship.

And so, you begin to accommodate even further in an attempt to cling to that person, that person who is the vessel of the feeling. And most likely, this other person is not one who responds well to clinginess.

And the cycle begins again. The person withdraws, and you push harder, and so on and so on.

And lo and behold, you are right back HOME AGAIN.

Except now you are even more depressed and hopeless than before.

You head to the roof and shout "Good God, how did I wind up back here again!" The pigeons scatter, bystanders pause to look up–and then the shame piles up. You feel powerless. You lose your self-respect. And your friends start to grumble about you being back in the same old place again (because people in this state do a great job of ignoring the healthy relationships and real support systems in their lives).

And as your authentic self becomes more and more displaced, you start to reach for the compensation that will make you feel okay–even if only for the moment.

And that's when the real downward spirals begin.

Compensation

The physics of the self is not unlike the physics of the universe: both abhor a vacuum. In the case of people, when the authentic self has been denied, our survival mechanism will kick in and seek out compensatory behaviors to fill the void.

When the self feels battered, misused, and even abused, it becomes preoccupied with finding security, safety, and relief. This is the cradle in which accommodation and addiction are born.

Many people have written about addiction, and I won't attempt an exhaustive examination of it here. But for the purposes of our discussion, it's helpful to think of addiction as a way of compensating for the loss of self.

And I'm not talking here only about the usual addictions: drugs, alcohol, gambling, sexual compulsions. While those are surely important, they manifest themselves in obvious ways that are relatively easy to detect.

Compensation for the loss of self also manifests in addictions that are more subtle but no less toxic than the ones that grab the headlines.

What I'm speaking of here is the addiction to the *known*, to the *familiar*. If addiction is the search for safety, then in the case of insecure attachment styles, addiction can be captured by this phrase: "I am safe with what I know. I am comfortable with the familiar and so I avoid the unknown and I do not strive to grow."

So, habits and patterns become the addiction: habits of overworking, overeating, hyperactivity, under-activity, procrastination and–yes–substance abuse. These habits present the illusion of comfort, of familiarity, but they are not your friends. In many cases, they keep you from leading a fulfilling life during which you achieve your true potential. In some cases, your habits can literally be killing you.

This is the conflict between the rational and irrational mind at its most stark. Because change is scary, because the unfamiliar is so intimidating, the power of an insecure attachment style will cause us to continue behavior that is literally life-threatening, rather than allowing us to take control of our lives and make positive, productive, and healthy changes to the way we do *everything*.

Who To Blame: No One, Sort Of

Is it fair that your childhood did not provide you an environment that allowed you to learn about yourself, to be accepted for yourself, to give you the ability to live with your actual self, rather than taking care of one or more of your world's grownups? Of course not.

But life is not fair.

Here's the thing. None of this is your fault.

Here's another thing. It's not your parents' fault either. As I mentioned, they did what they did, they were who they were, they are who they are.

Pointing the finger and affixing blame might feel good in the moment, but it doesn't solve the problem (and we're here to solve the problem). The truth is, no matter how much you chase your desire to repair your dysfunctional childhood, you cannot.

All the time and energy you pour into relationships that you subconsciously hope will be the one to expunge your upbringing are never going to change the past.

Because of emotional imprinting…because of our insecure attachment style…because of the power of the these deeply ingrained organizing patterns, the infant who became the child and the child who became the adult will still be subscribed to the same attachment style.

You will still be stuck in a pattern where getting it wrong equals getting it right–and vice versa.

You will continue to seek home…leading to relationships ending in frustration and the feeling of a life unlived–unless you decide to make a change. And I want you to change that equation.

And so, in order to turn your life around and swap out your dysfunctional choices for healthy ones, to replace your toxic relationships with mature, loving partnerships, to stop seeking home, you need to do something drastic.

Most people consider it very difficult. But I promise you, with effort and determination, you can do it.

You can leave home.

PART THREE:

SEEKING A NEW HOME

So far, I've explained that there are forces in our lives that are beyond our control–and that they will continue to exert a powerful influence over our lives until we decide to take control of them. That's what this section of the book is about.

Before we get to the How-To part of seeking a new home– of resetting your attachment style and allowing yourself to explode into a new world of self-control and fulfillment–I want to give you two ideas to keep in mind along the way.

Idea One: Improvement Feels Scary

Let me state this bluntly: by seeking a new home, you are setting out to improve your life.

I'll state this bluntly too: improvement can feel dangerous and risky and threatening.

As we've discussed, people with insecure attachment styles crave familiarity. Change means moving toward the unfamiliar, and for the insecurely attached this can feel deeply frightening.

And so, in urging you to move away from your original attachment style, I recognize that I am asking you to do something that is antithetical and potentially very painful for an insecurely attached person. And I want you to recognize it too.

As you forge ahead in your quest for improvement, I am going to ask you to take risks that, in the past, would have made you feel uncomfortable, or caused you emotional pain, even trauma. I am going to ask you to see that the world can be different from the one you grew up in. I am going to ask you to value yourself instead of over-accommodating others. I will encourage you to act in a way that is the opposite of what you feel and know.

And this may lead you to want to charge right back into your old way of life.

When those feelings arise, take a minute. Breathe deeply. Recognize them. And remind yourself that you can be against change all you want, but if you are, then you will lose.

Because change is a part of life. Hairstyles change, political regimes change, street names change, your favorite pizza place gets replaced by a high-rise condo…

Change happens all around us. To be against it is to be against life itself. On the other hand, if you ally and align yourself with change, you will be teaming up with the natural order of things.

That's empowering.

If and when you waver in your commitment to making change, remember that history, life and the universe all run on the power of change. Make it your own power source too.

Idea Two: Get Ready To Grieve

Another thing I will ask you to do as you reset your attachment style is, naturally, to say goodbye to your old one.

This can be tough. Your previous attachment style is one of the most ancient aspects of your psyche. For better or worse, it's tied up with all of your earliest life experiences, the people who knew you when you were at your most vulnerable and dependent–the original you.

Now you may be in a big hurry to say, "Good riddance to all that." In that case, the road to change will be smoother.

But for many people, letting go of their attachment style brings up deep feelings of sadness.

A friend of mine who gave up smoking after twenty years said that the hardest part was that it felt like "saying goodbye to his best friend." Exactly. As we saw earlier, attachment styles are closely associated with addictions large and small– and leaving addictions behind can be very, very emotionally difficult.

But grieving is an important part of growing. Because as bad as grieving can sometimes feel, the paradox is that failing to grieve feels even worse.

Nothing is more emotionally consuming than trying to ward off painful experiences from the past. By not grieving, you continue to re-live old ruptures and traumas and the original emotions that went along with those experiences.

And so, failure to grieve is associated with all kinds of compensatory behaviors like addictions, compulsions, bad choices–searching for self-soothing and longing for and seeking out others in the hope that they will provide what you are lacking–exactly the same kind of behaviors as the maladaptive attachment style you're trying to shake off in the first place.

Because of this, the grieving process is a vital part of growth.

And so…grieve. Experience things as they are, not as you wish they were. Acknowledge that you do not have other people under your control. Recognize angry feelings when they crop up; don't suppress them.

Most important–don't run away from yourself! Respect any scared, nervous, or sad feelings you may experience enough to examine them. Don't dismiss or bury them–that's what led to all the trouble in the first place.

* * *

I'll have more to say about these two ideas in the next section. For now, I want you to understand that leaving home–changing your attachment style–can require a leap of faith, and that faith can be tested as you grow and evolve.

Doubt, fear, mourning, grief–these emotions tempt us to run back to our old familiar patterns. Sometimes they crop up once a week. Sometimes they crop up once a minute.

Be strong. I believe in you. I believe in you because I have seen hundreds of people come through my door convinced that they could never turn their lives around. And then they've proceeded to turn their lives around.

If they can do it, you can too. And if I believe in you, even though I've never met you, then you can believe in yourself!

The payoff of this journey will be awesome, and well worth the effort it will take.

Real self-respect. Experiencing reality as you see it. Not having to accommodate the impossible demands of another. Being tethered to a person in ways that are healthy, positive, productive, and joyful…

If you are willing to confront difficult emotions for a time, to invite them in, experience them, reflect on them, and not see them as enemies but as allies in your quest to improve yourself and your circumstances, then all of these will be yours to enjoy.

Here's how to actually do it.

PART FOUR:

HOW TO FIX YOUR INSECURE ATTACHMENT STYLE

Turn Me Right Round / Do You Remember LP's

An LP record consists of one long groove on each side. When you play the same song over and over again on the album, a deeper groove can develop in a part of the main groove, and the needle will get stuck in it and it will start to skip, to repeat itself. To get unstuck and listen to the rest of the song, you have to push the needle out of the groove.

Your attachment style is like a skip in your life's record. It keeps sending you back to the same repetitive part of your life's groove, over and over again. You never getting to the rest of the album!

But with the cultivation of awareness, you can begin to notice that the same song is being played over and over again. And then you can learn how to give our life's record player a THWAP, and push the needle out of that same repetitive skip so you hear the rest of your life's music.

To make this change, I will teach you how to look at your emotions–and emotional impulses–from a new perspective, so you can see how your entrenched patterns influence your behavior and understand how to take back control over your choices and decisions.

But to really succeed, to really break away from those old patterns and launch yourself into a new and healthier approach to life, you'll need to marshal not only all your mental resources but your physical energy as well.

The dictatorial hold of your attachment style is strong. You'll need resolve and willpower to separate yourself from it. Your mind and your psyche will do the mental work. But your brain is your physical tool for getting better, and your body provides energy and support for your brain.

That's why we're going to attack your attachment style on two fronts: the mental *and* the physical. With your mind and body working in tandem, your old, unhealthy attachment style might put up a fight, but in the long run it won't have a chance.

The Body

Exercise

Brace yourself for a mind-blowing piece of advice: exercise is good.

Of course, you already know that. Your heart, your muscles, your hormones, your longevity–exercise benefits 'em all.

But don't worry, I'm not about to hand this part of the book over to Jane Fonda or the trainers from The Biggest Loser; I don't care how prominent your abs are or whether you can do one hundred pushups in one hundred seconds. What I want to talk about are the specific effects that exercise has on *mood*.

Changing your attachment style is not an overnight assignment. It requires energy and stamina, and there may very well be times when its hard to see the destination because of all the curves in the road.

That's why exercise is so important to the process. Exercise provides the energy you'll need to substantiate your life-changing efforts. It also injects quick jolts of positivity into your day, which come in handy during those times when the job of changing your life might seem to be more work than you can handle.

Exercise connects us to ourselves in a very real and visceral way. It gives us confidence and makes us feel stronger–both figuratively and literally. Exercise allows us to set and then accomplish a concrete goal, giving us bragging rights and a reason to feel proud.

The downside: many people view exercise with a sense of dread, and this is especially true of those with an insecure attachment style.

Remember, for the insecurely attached, anything that focuses attention on the self is deemed "bad," territory to be avoided. It's a threat to the childhood attachment "voice" that keeps screaming "focus on the other, not on yourself!"

The insecurely attached often let themselves avoid by giving up because they conclude that "I'm just a lazy person", when the truth is that they have learned that focusing on the self is dangerous and should be avoided. They turn the knowledge that exercise can make them feel better into an opening for self-criticism…echoing the sentiments that they were taught to hold about themselves from their earliest days.

But I am not going to let you off the hook so easily.

First of all, I'm not out to turn anyone into a record-breaking triathlete. (In fact, I'm not even going to prescribe specific exercises for you to do. We are steeped enough in the culture of exercise that I'm sure you can find an exercise regimen that's appropriate for you all on your own.)

Instead, I want you to exercise because of the physical benefits I've described, but most importantly because it represents a very clear, very simple yet very productive opportunity to start making choices that are good for *you*.

Exercise gives the insecurely attached person a chance to get their attention away from the "Other" for a few moments, and to put it on himself.

Exercise gives you the chance to do what's in your best interest. And it will show you that, rather than causing the world to come crashing down around you, doing things for yourself will actually be beneficial for you.

It also provides you with the opportunity to make contact with uncomfortable feelings, perhaps feelings of inertia, procrastination, or anxiety. And here is the good news: it is exactly these kinds of feelings that you want to make contact with, to be curious about and to get to know. To shed your old attachment style, you need to invite discomfort, to stop avoiding it. Exercise lets you do this in a very literal way.

Here are a few of the specific benefits you'll get by slipping on some spandex and running, riding, walking, hiking, swimming, surfing or parkour-ing your way to a healthier body.

- **Reduced Stress:** Exercise increases concentrations of norepinephrine, a chemical that can moderate the brain's response to stress.
- **Boost Happy Chemicals:** Research shows that a twenty-minute cardiovascular workout can enhance your mood for up to twelve hours. Exercise releases endorphins, which create feelings of happiness and euphoria. Studies have shown that exercise can even alleviate symptoms among the clinically depressed.
- **Improve Self-Confidence:** Regardless of weight, size, gender or age, exercise can quickly elevate a person's perception of his or her attractiveness.

- **Prevent Cognitive Decline:** Working out boosts the chemicals in the brain that support and prevent degeneration of the hippocampus, an important part of the brain for memory and learning.
- **Alleviate Anxiety:** The warm and fuzzy chemicals that are released during and after exercise can help people feel calmer.
- **Kick-up Brainpower:** Studies suggest that a good workout increases levels of a brain-derived protein (known as BDNF) in the body, believed to help with decision making, higher thinking and learning.
- **Help Control Addictions:** The brain releases dopamine, the "reward chemical" in response to any form of pleasure, be it exercise, sex, drugs, alcohol, or food. Unfortunately, some people become addicted to dopamine and dependent on the substances that produce it. Replace the dopamine source with exercise and see the rewards!
- **Increase Relaxation:** A moderate workout can be the equivalent of a sleeping pill for people with insomnia. Moving around five to six hours before bedtime raises the body's core temperature. When the body temp drops back to normal a few hours later, it signals the body that it's time to sleep.
- **Get More Done:** Stuck on a problem? The solution might be just a short walk or jog away. Research shows that workers who take time for exercise on a regular basis are more productive and have more energy.
- **Tap into Creativity:** A heart-pumping gym session can boost creativity for up to two hours afterwards.

- **Focus**: One other aspect of exercise that makes it beautiful: it allows you to focus on specific thoughts and feelings, and to let all your thoughts go completely.

For me, exercise is my day's best opportunity to be completely in the present. When I'm playing tennis, I find that my mind is totally occupied by the task at hand. Everything else fades away, and for those sixty minutes, it's just me and the game. Beyond the physical benefits of the workout, playing tennis shows me very clearly that it is possible for me to focus on what I'm doing–and only what I'm doing–for a prolonged amount of time.

Knowing that I can do it, I then try to apply that same level of focus to other things I do during the day: work, being with my family, writing and so on. I'm not always perfect at it, but thanks to tennis, I know what that kind of focus feels like, and I have something to aim for in other areas of my life.

Jogging, on the other hand, is exercise that I don't have to think about. I know my routes by heart, so I can let my brain wander wherever it wants to. I've come up with some of my best ideas while jogging. I've also had imaginary arguments, planned a party, thought about my marriage and other relationships, hummed songs, and let my mind go completely blank.

My point here is that exercise provides an opportunity to work out your brain as well. Rare indeed are the opportunities we have to both focus intensely and to give our brains a chance for unstructured play. Exercise offers both.

Finally, exercise gives us a chance to be completely in control. No one is going to do it for you. No one is going to make you do it. It's all up to you. You can see this as a reason to duck out. Or you can seize the opportunity to take control of this one aspect of your life. If you do, you will begin to notice an immediate shift in your self-esteem.

And each time you are able to "be with" your feelings of inertia, or dread, of resistance to change (all feelings that an insecurely attached person experiences when focusing on herself) and then *not give in* to those feelings, but instead make a healthy alternative choice, you will be building parts of yourself. You will change the neurological pathways in your brain, getting out of your well-worn mental ruts and your brain's addiction to doing things the old way.

It might seem daunting. It might seem exhausting. But I guarantee you, if you start to change these patterns, if you move toward your discomfort rather than away from it, and if you are disciplined about it, you will begin to create an entirely new reality for yourself, one where you are in control for a change.

You will begin to free yourself from the shackles of your past patterns. You will feel like you should be proud of yourself–and you'll be right.

Sleep

Remember when I said that your brain is your tool for getting better? Well, as you go about changing your old patterns and building your new approach to life, you want that tool to be as sharp and effective as possible. And there is no tool more effective than sleep.

Much has been written–and more is being discovered every day–about how much sleep Americans aren't getting…and how important sleep is to our physical and mental health.

That's why I want you to make a pointed effort to get enough good sleep every night. With a solid and healthy night's sleep under your belt, you'll be able to view your choices with the clarity, acuity, and perspective you need. Without a good night's sleep, you'll be at an automatic disadvantage and far more susceptible to slipping back into old patterns– because avoiding change takes far less energy and mental commitment than making it.

But get ready, because sleeping well is not something that the insecurely attached tend to be particularly good at. Why? Because sleep is about letting go, surrendering to our environment…and this is in direct contrast to what the insecurely attached have been taught.

Remember, for the insecurely attached, it's all about being aware of the *Other*, to service their needs, to provide for them. So, the idea of going to sleep and turning off the radar, of being unaware of those around us, is in opposition to our ingrained reflexes.

This is a drag, because the insecurely attached tend to end the day in an exhausted state, drained from all the energy they expend in managing others.

But instead of tucking in for a good night of restorative sleep, you stay up watching TV, or you surf the web, searching for something fulfilling–and of course TV and the internet aren't going to provide it.

So, you get into a vicious cycle: the search for fulfillment at the end of the night ends badly, a good night's restorative sleep is lost, you're wiped out the next day, and you lack the mental clarity to make any but the most reflexive choices.

Ugh!

And if that's not enough, here are some the other consequences of poor sleep:

Sleep Loss Impairs Judgment

- Lack of sleep can affect our interpretation of events. This hurts our ability to make sound judgments because we may not assess situations accurately and act on them wisely.
- According to a 2004 study, people who sleep less than six hours a day were almost 30% more likely to become obese than those who slept seven to nine hours. Not only does sleep loss appear to stimulate appetite, it also stimulates cravings for high-fat, high-carbohydrate foods.

Sleepiness Makes You Forgetful

- In 2009, American and French researchers determined that brain events called "sharp wave ripples" are responsible for consolidating memory. The ripples also transfer learned information from the hippocampus to the neocortex of the brain, where long-term memories are stored. Sharp wave ripples occur mostly during the deepest levels of sleep– exactly what you're *not* getting if you're not sleeping well.

Lack of Sleep Kills Sex Drive

- Sleep specialists say that sleep-deprived men and women report lower libidos and less interest in sex. Depleted energy, sleepiness, and increased tension may be largely to blame.

Sleep Loss Dumbs You Down

- Sleep plays a critical role in thinking and learning. Lack of sleep hurts these cognitive processes in many ways. Sleep deprivation impairs attention, alertness, concentration, reasoning, and problem solving. This makes it more difficult to learn efficiently.
- There is a host of research demonstrating that the restorative effects of sleep on the brain and body depend on seven to nine hours of healthy sleep. Current research is finding loss of sleep associated with long term cognitive impairment, and–again–since your brain is your tool for getting better, it is very important for you to make choices that will give you a good night of sack time.

Here are a few tips to get you started on your way to a healthy night in dreamland (ten minutes on the Internet will give you dozens more):

Tips for a Healthy Night's Sleep:

- Research shows that using a smartphone, tablet, or computer with normal brightness before bedtime reduces levels of melatonin (an important sleep-related hormone) and makes it more difficult to fall asleep. Get an app (e.g., flux) that changes the brightness of your computer or phone as evening falls so that you're not staring at an ultra-bright screen right before bedtime.

- Even better than tweaking your electronics: just turn 'em off, at least one hour before going to bed. It might be tough, but try it for a week. If you don't see results, I will eat my hat.
- Read a book before you go to bed. Reading connects you to yourself in ways that TV watching and web surfing never will. Reading goes deep into the experiential parts of the brain, connecting you to complex thoughts and emotions, leaving you feeling connected to yourself and others.
- Do not eat a full meal before going to bed. The work of digesting that meal keeps your body from fully relaxing.
- Don't consume alcohol before going to bed. It might seem like alcohol helps make you feel sleepy, but the truth is that, after an initial downturn in energy, the carbs in booze, along with its tendency to make you get up to use the bathroom, will put the kibosh on a good night's sleep.
- Sleep cool. Keep temperature in your bedroom around sixty-five degrees, and pile on the blankets if you must. A cooler room stimulates a better night's sleep.

One last benefit of changing your sleep pattern: as with exercise, these are decisions and alterations that you are making. They represent opportunities to take control of your choices, rather than leaving those choices to your old reflexes. Setting the conditions necessary for a good night's sleep might cause you to do away with some things you hold dear and this might make you feel anxious or bring up feelings of loss.

But we want to invite those feelings. They might not be comfortable, but the whole idea here is to shatter our presumptions about what feels normal and comfortable. Remember, we are welcoming the uncomfortable feelings that will come when we decide to make healthy choices. We invite them into our consciousness with patience curiosity and compassion as a way of confronting and moving beyond the feelings of discomfort healthy choices produce.

Make the hard choices. Take ownership of them. Don't look for the answers outside yourself. You can do it. Turn off the TV for a week, avoid that late night snack before bedtimes–don't let these things define you and the way you live. Instead, confront the fear you have about making these changes…and then make them anyway.

Do it right, do it with conviction, and you will feel like a new person–because you will be.

Diet

And now we come to a gigantic bugaboo for the majority of Americans: the foods we decide to put into our mouths every day, and from which we are meant to draw merely sustenance, but which instead provide too many of us with our emotional and psychic sense of well-being. In a word: diet.

But brace yourself: I'm going to keep this section short, partly because so much has been written about diet elsewhere that if you put it all end to end, you could walk on it from your living room to your refrigerator for the rest of time. If you want to dig into nutrition in depth, I refer you to the websites of the American Medical Association (ama-assn.org) and the American Nutrition Association (http://americannutritionassociation.org/) as starting points.

But I'm also going to keep it short here because I've got some particular words to say about food in the next section. For now, insofar as diet pertains to keeping your body healthy and strong and serving as a powerful support system for the life-changing work of abandoning your old attachment style, I'll simply offer this basic common-sense advice:

- Rid your home of junk food and snacks so they won't be around when you're tempted.
- Place healthy foods (bananas and apples, say) out on the counter and in your line of sight.
- Do snack–but eat healthy snacks. Don't let yourself get too hungry…because hungry people tend to make terrible short-sighted choices (both with food and other things).
- Permanently eliminate one processed food from your diet per year (e.g., hot dogs this year, candy corn next year)
- When choosing foods, ask yourself: "Would I feed this to my child?" If the answer is no, then don't feed it to yourself.
- Detox from sugar, caffeine, and refined carbohydrates.

As you free yourself from your dependence on (or addiction to) these substances, you will reassert your sense of control over your diet. Giving up foods can feel depriving and anxiety producing–but again take advantage of changes by inviting and being curious about the feelings that emerge when you make healthy choices around food. Keep in mind we are focusing on the discomfort of healthy choices, we are inviting this discomfort into our awareness, finally making space for it, getting to know it, being curious about it. (And as you pursue a healthier diet, even as healthy choices make you emotionally uncomfortable, try to stay aware of how much better you will begin to feel physically.)

The Mind

The Importance of Self-Awareness

And now we turn to the star of the whole attachment style show: the mind.

This is where the main action will play out, the drama (and occasional comedy) that will unfold as you leave behind your old patterns and habits and embark on a new and healthier way of living your life.

Up to now, I've armed (or possibly bombarded) you with information about what goes into an attachment style, how an unhealthy attachment style can affect your life, why to change it, and how to physically prepare yourself for the journey.

As complex as the body is, the mind is vastly more nuanced and mysterious. Yet for all its complications–and for all the information that I've provided you with so far–making the mental and emotional adjustments necessary to move beyond your unhealthy attachment style really requires that you understand only one more concept: self-awareness.

Everything in this section revolves in some way around the idea of self-awareness. Everything has been leading up to this, and from here on out it's what we're all about: self-awareness. That means you developing the ability to observe your own behavior from a distance...to assess your choices critically–but not judgmentally...to see yourself as others see you...to realize that you are in charge of what you do and the actions you take...and then to act on that realization by making healthier, more productive and more positive choices as you go through life.

Let's get started.

Me, Myself, and I / The Trifecta of Connectedness

Being self-aware means having the ability to step outside yourself to observe yourself and your behavior, both in the long term and in the moment.

Developing self-awareness will resonate in all aspects of your life. But since we're here primarily to break your unhealthy attachment styles hold on you so you can work on your ability to develop functional and fulfilling relationships, let's start with the first relationship you need to repair: your relationship to yourself.

In its most literal sense, self-awareness allows you to assess your behavior and attitudes honestly and realistically. That's why developing it is so crucial to your ability to break with your attachment style.

When people are mired in their insecure attachment style, they lack the ability to truly examine both their behavior and the world at large because they are stuck in their deeply ingrained repetitive patterns.

But by changing the way we see ourselves, by developing the ability to watch ourselves as we go through our days and our lives, we can change our relationship to our problems and our patterns. We provide ourselves, through our ability to self-reflect, the distance we need to take control of our lives through the new kinds of choices we make.

By becoming aware of ourselves and our experiences, we actively give ourselves space to make choices that we previously would not have made. We learn to recognize when our life record, our LP, is skipping, and we see that we need to THWAP it to get it to moving along.

The cool thing is, even the smallest amount of self-awareness can give rise to an intuition or insight that can be transformative.

Here's what I mean.

One day, my wife and I were having lunch, and she started talking about her mother. When my wife discusses emotional subjects, she tends to become very detailed. I, by nature, tend to listen to the emotional dimension of things. So as my wife became more literal and detail oriented, I began to feel frustrated and distracted by all the data she was delivering. To me, she was making the story needlessly complicated.

I began feeling tense and distracted, and I started wishing my wife would communicate more clearly. I was on the verge of telling her to focus on the substance and not worry about the logistics of the situation she was describing–and suddenly I stopped.

I asked myself: "What would I hope to accomplish with that comment?" All that would happen, I realized, is that my wife would become defensive and tell me that I wasn't listening to her–and she'd be right! Because I wasn't listening to her. Instead, I was getting angry because she wasn't telling me what I wanted to hear.

And I realized: "Hey, if I am really listening to her, if I am really seeing her, I would recognize that this is how she talks when she is dealing with emotional issues, this is how she handles her emotionality. If I was really being with her, I would see her for who she is at this moment, not from the perspective of who I want her to be or wished she was."

I then thought: "And why do I wish she was this other way?"

This insight of self-awareness–of how I was turning her way of talking into something that had more to do with me than with her–was really important. And it happened in a flash, such that I was able to relax and let her finish talking exactly as she wished.

This *"Why am I feeling this?"* inquiry is an extremely important kind of question to be able to ask yourself (and it can take practice to get into the habit of asking it). This question is important not so much for the answer but for the recognition that what you are feeling is filtered through your own subjective experience based on your own emotional needs in the moment–and the recognition that these emotional needs obscure your ability to really be with and hear the other.

The flash of insight I had was possible because I have developed–through years of false starts and sometimes painful experiences–the ability to examine myself from a distance.

There it is in a nutshell. Self-awareness: The ability to know when to stop and observe yourself.

In this case, I recognized that I was getting emotionally worked up–angry–at my wife for doing something she needed to be doing, for being who she is. I decided to stop needing her to be different, and I began to hear her for who she was at that very moment. And I began to feel more warmly toward her.

Instead of getting annoyed because of my own difficulty in sitting with my own feelings of frustration, by noticing and focusing on my inner experience, I was able to respond to my wife in ways that previously would not have been available to me. In the end:

1. My wife felt listened to
2. I felt like a loving and competent husband, and
3. My wife felt appreciative toward me for being heard.

I call this The Trifecta of Connectedness: I am connected to myself, therefore I can be present for others in attuned ways, and in return they feel heard and express their love and appreciation back to me. Everyone wins!

This is the power of self-awareness, of self-observation, and it's one of the main tools we need in breaking away from our attachment styles.

Here is how to begin to achieve it.

Meet Your Mind

The main way to cultivate self-awareness is to develop a tool commonly known as "mindfulness."

Before we get into the steps involved with this, I'd like to say a word in mindfulness's defense. In my opinion the term "mindfulness" still suffers unfairly because of its association with untested, untethered and even hippy dippy practices, but current research has proven a correlation between mindfulness and positive mental health.

For me, mindfulness merely means taking some time out of your day to practice a few simple techniques that will help you to self-reflect and cultivate self-awareness.

What happens when you cultivate mindfulness? For one, you start to *notice* thoughts, feelings, and sensations in your body. These thoughts and feelings have always been there, but they have never had the time and space to be focused on. You may then notice how your thoughts spark certain emotions. These emotions may range from pleasant to unpleasant, to overwhelming. You may then notice how you react to these emotions; You may judge them. They may make you uncomfortable. You may want to get away from them, or you may want to hold onto them. These initial reactions are usually reflexive and automatic.

If you stick with it, in time, you will develop the ability to observe yourself–a part of you will notice how these reflexive feelings and thoughts have come to define you. With time, you will begin to invite feelings and thoughts and sensations that you had previously shied away from. As you become curious and compassionate to these parts of you, you will come to a deeper understanding yourself, and with that, you will naturally become more accepting of yourself. You will, in fact, become able to be with yourself! And because of that simple but profound fact, you will want to surround yourself with people who also want to be with you.

And here's an added benefit: it's really relaxing! And it can sharpen your mind a rejuvenate your day.

What follows are the customized exercises I use to achieve mindfulness. I do a little bit of this every day–sometimes as much as twenty minutes, sometimes as few as five. The amount of time you spend matters less than consistency and commitment.

It might seem weird, it might give you the heebie-jeebies, but please give mindfulness a chance. Seriously, what have you got to lose? I promise it really is one of the best ways out there to get in touch with what your body and mind are actually experiencing.

In fact, that's the whole point. If you are feeling scared, nervous, or intimidated as you go through this exercise, I want you to sit with that. For now, don't try to figure out *why* you feel that way. Just live with it. Because that act alone– that inviting in of all the feelings you experience and not running away from them–represents the kind of change you need to make to develop self-awareness, to learn what you're really feeling, and to break away from your attachment style.

And the more you do that, the more you will develop a thorough understanding of yourself–and the more you'll be able to be truly and confidently yourself around a romantic interest.

So, give this a fair shot. Do it five minutes a day for a week. I promise, if you have the right attitude, the results will speak for themselves.

Exercise To Achieve Mindfulness:

Sit comfortably

Take three slow deep but natural breaths

Bring your attention to your breath and only your breath. Focus on the fact that you are breathing. Notice your nostrils, your abdomen, and the entire movement of your breath through your body.

When you find yourself distracted by a sound or sensation or, most important, a thought, don't fight it. Instead, notice it. Notice that your mind has wandered from your breath. Then gently return to the focus of your breath.

Those are the basics. Yep, that's basically it!

Your mind will wander a lot, especially early on as you learn to practice mindfulness, and you may have many uncomfortable sensations. Don't judge those distractions. Be patient. Keep at it, and mindfulness will be yours.

And as you keep at it, bear this in mind:

Notice how much preconception you bring to this breathing exercise. Don't judge it! Just bring your attention back to your breathing.

Trust yourself.

Do not strive! Do not try! That's right. Mindfulness is about "non-doing." It's about being with, right here, right now. Remember, you are simply allowing anything and everything that you experience from moment to moment to be here. The invitation is to be with it, to embrace it and not to do anything with it. Just be aware.

Acceptance: take each moment in your breathing session as it comes, not as you hope or wished or thought it should. Whatever you feel, notice it. I can guarantee you that whatever you are feeling or thinking will change from one moment to the next. Give yourself a chance to experience that.

Letting go: you will notice that your mind will cling to certain thoughts and ideas, both negative and positive. That's totally cool. In pursuing mindfulness, we don't invite good feelings and reject bad ones, we just let them be what they are, we observe them. If they are particularly sticky, we can notice what it feels like to hold on to them. Once you have noticed the feeling, again, return your attention to your breathing.

Okay, you've completed one mindfulness session–or hopefully a week's worth. What did you just learn?

Just this: an insecure attachment style keeps us from focusing on our true selves. It commands us to look away from our needs, our reality, and focus on pursuing others.

Practicing mindfulness gives us the chance–possibly for the first time in our lives–to focus not on someone else but on what *we* are thinking and feeling. And it further tells us that, whatever our thoughts and feelings, it is okay not to judge them.

This is the opposite of what our attachment style tells us. An insecure attachment style causes you to shun your own deepest thoughts and feelings by making you feel ashamed of them, by urging you to ignore and bury them.

Practicing mindfulness is crucial to experiencing what it's like to think a real thought and have a real feeling *without feeling bad about it, without dismissing it or judging it.* Mindfulness lets us know that it's okay to be ourselves. Which, as I've said, is step number one in developing the ability to be with someone else.

(If you want to read up more on mindfulness and mindful meditation, there are plenty of resources out there. In particular I recommend Jon-Kabat Zinn's "Full Catastrophe Living" and Google guru Chade-meng Tan's "Search Inside Yourself.")

In essence, mindfulness is the crucial second part of putting yourself in charge of your decisions, instead of your attachment style. Self-awareness gives us the ability to see ourselves; mindfulness gives us the ability to be with ourselves.

The next step is to take charge of the things we *do*. This is where the physical, mental, and emotional preparation we've done so far really starts to pay off. Thought patterns and internal instincts are important. But it is through our actions that we interact with the world.

And ultimately, it's our actions that we're out to change as we prepare ourselves to enter lasting, fulfilling relationships. And as you seek the ability to truly share yourself with someone else in honest and healthy ways, I suggest that you begin this most significant of journeys by focusing on a timeless talisman of profound healing and self-empowerment.

RESET YOUR ROMANTIC GPS

Ladies and gentlemen, I give you: The Pepperoni Project.

PART FIVE:

CHOICES

The Pepperoni Project

Part of what makes our attachment styles difficult to break away from is the power they have to dictate our choices in life. We think that free will is what separates us from the chimpanzees and elephants, lynxes and narwhals of the world. But the fact is, our attachment styles are like the Song of the Sirens, calling us home, directing us, whispering in our ears, telling us what to do and who to find attractive every minute of the day.

Changing your attachment style means taking back control over the pivotal choices in your life. And you must start somewhere. So how about pizza?

I pick pizza because pizza is my thing. If pizza is not your thing, please select an appropriate substitute–Chinese food, ice cream, chips, fries–as you read through the following exercise and learn how to take charge of your decision making.

The Pull Of The Trigger

Food is an essential building block in our tower of self-awareness, because for the vast majority of people, food is not just a source of nutrition, it's a source of meaning. Our relationship to food can tell us a great deal about ourselves, if we are willing to listen.

Many people associate certain emotions with food. They self-medicate with food, they calm themselves with food, they soothe themselves with it. They imbue food with the power of emotional regulation.

When the emotional pressure is on, when certain triggers have been pulled, people crave certain foods both physiologically and psychologically in hopes that these foods will fill a void, satisfy a hunger, and do emotional things for us. People in this state confuse emotional need with the feeling of physical hunger.

Learning to recognize these triggers, becoming aware of them, is a vital skill to develop and practice as we increase our self-awareness and ability to make our own choices in life.

And so…

Be Brave: Ask Why You Crave

Cravings

Cravings for food are one of our most potent clues that something fishy is going on with our emotional lives. One of the things that makes cravings such slippery little devils is that we often don't recognize our cravings as cravings. We think of them more as a part of us, as something that defines us. Most of us are so habituated to our cravings and longings that we cannot tell the difference between what we crave and who we are.

"It's not that I crave pepperoni pizza," the thinking goes, "it's that I am a pepperoni pizza lover!"

Really? Is that who you are? Because I think there's more to you than that.

Cravings are not inherently bad. In fact, cravings are like your psyche's early warning system. They're trying to tell us something. They're saying: "Pay attention! Something is not balanced!"

The message is important–but it takes self-awareness to hear it. And responding to cravings is a vital step in learning to take back control of the way we make decisions (both the day-to-day variety and the life altering ones). I call this response the Pepperoni Project.

Here's how the Pepperoni Project works.

Say you're craving a pepperoni pizza. You know the drill: you've been thinking about it. Looking forward to it. Maybe even dreaming about it. But before you pick up the phone or get online to order it...stop.

Take a moment to be present and notice your craving. Notice how urgent the craving feels. Does it feel like nothing else in the world could possibly satisfy that craving? Feel that. Does it seem like the world will come crashing down–or that you'll at least be sorely disappointed–if you can't have your pepperoni pizza? Feel that.

Now recognize how much power you are handing over to this little puck of meat on a pizza. You may think something like: "Wow, this pepperoni really has a grip on me. It feels like nothing is more important to me, at this moment, than getting pizza with pepperoni."

You feel like you really, really need it. That you deserve it. That you have to have it.

Now sit with that feeling. –Just recognize it in yourself.

Notice, please, that I haven't said "Don't order the pizza" or "Get the pizza but leave off the pepperoni." All I want you to do is pause and recognize that you have imbued this pepperoni with a lot of power and responsibility for your happiness and fulfillment at this moment.

You might not see it as life and death, but this craving does have the ability to determine your happiness–even if just for a few moments.

Think about that. Then notice if your relationship to the pepperoni has shifted.

First of all, you might be surprised to think of yourself as being in a relationship with the pepperoni. But the fact is that, for the time being, you are! And the pepperoni is the one who's calling the shots! It's the one who's going to determine your happiness in this moment.

Reflect on that idea. It's a powerful idea. And now notice: have your feelings about this pepperoni shifted? Are you experiencing the craving in the same way?

The pepperoni–an innocent bystander in all this–hasn't changed. What has changed is your recognition that your craving of it is reflexive. By which I mean that your craving is so powerful, it has taken the idea of CHOICE right out of the equation. A moment or two ago, you HAD to have pepperoni–there were no two ways about it.

But then you realize that–wait a minute–I am a grown-up human being, and I can order a pizza any way I want.

All of a sudden, the possibilities of how you can respond to this craving of yours have expanded. Now you can go ahead and order your pepperoni pizza–but you can do so because you've taken a thoughtless reflex and shifted it into the realm of CHOICE–a choice which embodies thought and reflection and awareness.

This is an extremely simple and mundane exercise, but the lesson it contains is fundamental. *Shifting the decisions we make from the realm of reflex to the realm of choice is vital to the process of leaving home.*

Once you stop and think about that pepperoni pizza, I guarantee that you will enjoy it more and be more present when you eat it.

And the next time you order pepperoni pizza, go a step further. Before you order it, think about eating the pepperoni. Ask yourself: How will I feel afterwards? How many slices will I eat? Is it good for me? Is it really what I need or want, or is it a substitute for something else?

In important ways, the answers to these questions matter much less than the fact that you are asking them. The point here is to take an *observing stance* on something you used to do without thinking about it.

This is just an exercise, but the metaphor is profound. What other cravings do we have? And how often do we let them lead us around by the collar? Do we feel like we deserve them? Do we feel somehow wronged if we don't get them?

By becoming self-aware, by learning to observe our behavior non-judgmentally but honestly, we can become our own decision-makers, no longer under the sway of our compulsions, our unmet needs–and our insecurely attached childhoods.

The minute you become an observer of your life, you develop a relationship with yourself that you never had before. As you begin to develop awareness of the deeply ingrained patterns that organize your life, you move from living in and recreating the past to the actual present. It is from this position, a position of awareness and connectedness with yourself, that you can then begin to perceive your overall world.

When you view your world from a state a connectedness, you will stop making decisions based on longing. Being connected to yourself allows you to feel more stabilized and regulated, so the pepperoni stops being the repository of all your momentary hopes and needs.

The Big Shift

Now for the big shift: think about substituting a person for the pepperoni.

Think about what it would be like to experience your relationships not through the lens of an insecure attachment in which you need people to satisfy your unconscious, reflexive cravings and longings–but from the perspective of a more balanced self, a self that has power over its choices, a power developed through your connectedness to yourself.

A while back, the Magic Eye book enjoyed a moment in the spotlight. Perhaps you remember these books. They showed pictures that appeared to be two-dimensional renderings of abstract images…but when you stared at them long enough and in the right way–WHAMMO! Suddenly a 3D picture emerged, and it was revelatory. It came with a moment of deep satisfaction, and a lesson: you can stare at something a long time, but only when you shift your perspective will you see the picture that has been there all along.

"Now I get it!" is the feeling you'd experience when you first saw the 3D image. This is the feeling I want you to experience regarding your choices in life, both culinary and romantic.

Whether it's pizza or people, when we shift from our insecure attachment style, we can begin to see the things we desire for what or who they are, and not what we need them to be. We can stop elevating people or being so disappointed in them.

When you understand the romantic choices you make in the same terms as ordering a certain kind of pizza, the inappropriate partner you would have gone for in the past stops being the repository of all your hopes for a magically beautiful life. Your typical love object starts to lose his or her power of seduction; their ability to seem more powerful than you diminishes.

There is nothing wrong with needing. What we do want to do away with, though, is desperation–and our tendency to confuse the two.

When you are present and in the moment, when you are self-aware, you see reality for what it is. You can be more of your authentic self. And because you feel anchored to life through your relationship with yourself–a position that naturally provides greater confidence and self-reliance–you are able to view others more generously and less judgmentally.

If you are with someone who is wrong for you, you will see them for who they are and find the strength to let them go. And when you are with someone who is right for you, you will experience the trifecta of connectedness.

It's not easy to do this, and it might sound like a huge leap.

The good news is that the best tools for cultivating awareness are free. And once you get the hang of it, the hang of noticing the difference between your thoughts and yourself, you will see that our daily lives offer us enormous learning opportunities, opportunities that are meaningful and fun.

That's why I suggest you start with the pizza. It may seem silly but ask any pilot or sailor–on a long journey, the tiniest little change in course makes a huge difference in where you eventually wind up.

So, start small. Think about little cravings and compulsions. Take back the power you've given them.

If you are disciplined, if you create and cultivate awareness, if you pay attention to yourself and your patterns, if you make these little course corrections, you will end up in a totally different place than you ever expected. And it will be a far better place than the one you were in before.

RESET YOUR ROMANTIC GPS

Take A Different Road

Part of changing your attachment style is to shake up your daily routine and upend your way of doing things. Most of doing this involves work you need to do on yourself–but not all of it.

One tip I give to a lot of my patients: download the smartphone travel and navigation app WAZE. This is not an advertisement!

Waze is a great teacher for the insecurely attached. Insecurely attached people covet the known, the familiar. They like reliability, they steer clear of surprises even if those surprises are good for them.

And the more this person goes for the known, the more they take the familiar road, the more their muscles atrophy, and the more dependent on familiarity they become. This is where WAZE comes in.

WAZE detects the fastest route to take to get from Point A to Point B. Sometimes it will be the road you're used to taking. But a lot of times WAZE will send you a different way–sometimes even on back streets that you've never heard of. WAZE will show you how to avoid traffic jams and accidents–but you have to trust it and go off of your familiar route.

For the insecurely attached person who is afraid of the new, it can be a battle, but if you surrender to it, WAZE will not let you down. When you follow WAZE, it will take you places that you may have passed hundreds of times but never explored, through neighborhoods that you never know existed, nice neighborhoods and maybe not so nice neighborhoods.

You will discover many new things that were always there, but that you never focused on before. It will expand your surroundings. And the best part is that if you miss a street because you were distracted by something you've never seen before, WAZE will reset its bearings and get you back on the path. For the insecurely attached, WAZE is like having a trusted tour guide who helps you realize that it's okay to wander off your familiar path.

I love the beaten path when I'm driving. I do not like to veer away from it. But WAZE asks me to veer all the time–and each time I do, I am reminded of how much I pass by every day that I am not paying attention to, and how nice it is to experience new places and new terrain.

Mindfulness does the same thing. It leads you to discover that these kinds of experiences are all around us. Mindfulness makes the mundane much more dimensional and colorful and meaningful, and life in general becomes much more interesting as we begin to let go of our reflexive assumptions, behaviors, and anxieties, and live a life where we pay attention, get to know ourselves and learn how to take real care of ourselves.

PART SIX:

BEING WITH OTHERS

Okay, so far, you've learned about attachment styles. You've developed an understanding of how they operate and why it's important to change an unhealthy attachment style. We've discussed the importance of a healthy body in making this major psychological shift. You've learned how to start training your brain to become aware of your own behavioral patterns. And you've begun doing exercises to gain the kind of perspective and awareness you need to take control of your choices in life.

To sum up: You've learned to be a fully activated person who is the master of her own actions, and who has the confidence and self-esteem to forge healthy relationships with other people who are suited for you–possibly for the first time in your life.

Great! And now that you've learned to be with yourself for real, it's time for the big lasagna: being with someone else.

Yep, you've met someone, you like 'em, and it's time to be with 'em. The self-awareness, the healthiness, the confidence, the empowerment…this is where it all comes together. It's relationship time.

And now that you're perfect, it's time to start making mistakes.

Which is just another way of saying: let's get real. It's terrific that you are now your own person in a way that you never have been before. But as you are no doubt aware, there is no such thing as a 100% perfect relationship. Conflicts will arise. Differences of opinion. Incompatible goals.

The difference–the HUGE difference–is that now you are in a position to approach these challenges from a position of power and confidence, with the ability to take the other person's point of view into account without feeling a desperate need to accommodate that person at all costs.

You are ready to enter the world of real, mature, mutually loving relationships. Luckily, the work you've done so far will stand you in good stead as you finally make healthy, appropriate room in your life for someone else.

Here's how to apply some of what you're learned about yourself to a relationship with someone else.

Listening

Earlier we discussed the importance of being able to listen to your own thoughts and feelings as they're happening. The same holds true for your relationship with someone else.

Listening is one of the most fundamental skills that a person can bring to a relationship, but it's a skill that many people seem to lack. Remember my description of the meal I had with my wife a few sections back? My initial lack of real listening brought me perilously close to an unnecessary martial blow-up…and I'm a pro!

The good news is there are skills that can teach us how to listen and help us become disciplined listeners (and we can learn a lot about ourselves in the process).

Here's an exercise that will give you and your partner an express-entry passport into the wonderful world of listening.

Listen Up

You can tell when it's about to happen. Your partner says something. You tense up. You inhale sharply. You open your mouth to object…and are about to change a conversation into an argument or a confrontation of five-alarm conflagration.

Next time you find yourself in that situation, for your own sake and the good of your relationship, convince your partner to join you in this exercise:

1. Stop
2. Take three deep breaths
3. Choose one of you to go first (let's use the names "John" and "Jane" in our example below)
4. Jane says exactly what she wants to say, what she is thinking and feeling, to John.
5. Jane then asks John to repeat back to her what he heard her say. Not, mind you, what John feels or what John thinks, but just what John heard Jane say.
6. If John does not get it right in the judgment of Jane, then John has to keep trying.
7. If John wants help, he can ask Jane to clarify.
8. When John gets it right, Jane says yes that is how I felt and that is what I meant.

9. Now reverse it. Change roles. John expresses how he felt about what Jane originally said and about the issue at hand.
10. Jane now repeats back to John exactly what he said, trying over and over until she gets it right.
11. When Jane gets it right, John lets her know.

Congratulations! That is the end of the exercise. You have successfully heard and been heard! The conversation ends there. And the cool thing is, there is no right and no wrong. The lesson here: no one's opinion counts for more than another's. There are two subjective experiences at work here–and the job of the couple in these situations is to be able to appreciate that two subjectivities exist. Once that happens, it is much easier to work out a mutually acceptable solution to the problem.

Do this exercise whenever you get into a knot with your partner, and before long, you both will begin to notice that much of what you bring to a discussion–and what you anticipate the other person bringing–actually obscures your ability to hear the other.

Mindful Conversing

Bonus tip: cultivate mindfulness while conversing.

Any time you are in a conversation, practice your mindfulness techniques. Focus on the conversation. If you find your mind wandering, notice that, and bring your attention back to the speaker. Notice any sensations in your body, and then come back to giving the speaker your full attention. If you have the urge to correct them or to focus on yourself, notice that. Do not judge yourself and gently bring your attention back to the speaker.

Never Worry Alone

Part of learning to be in an honest, mature relationship is cultivating the ability to share your concerns and worries with your partner.

This can be tough for some people and downright scary for others, primarily because it makes people feel vulnerable.

This is understandable–but hey, part of the point of being in a relationship is so that you don't have to navigate life's choppier waters alone! And if you're doing things right, you shouldn't have to.

That's why one of the fundamental pieces of advice I give to patients who are in relationships is: never worry alone.

Voice your concerns, your fears, your hopes, and your dreams to your partner. If you do, you will notice something very peculiar happening: your fears and concerns will suddenly seem much smaller. They won't necessarily go away; bad news or a realistic worry will sometimes crop up and need handling. But the simple act of airing out a fear has the effect of diminishing it. And sharing it with your partner almost always brings the two of you closer–and if it doesn't, then sharing your concerns will teach you a lot about how suited your partner is for you.

This is partly because sharing your worries shows your partner that you respect him and honor him enough to seek out his counsel–or at least use him as a sounding board. It also reinforces the idea to your partner that you are conducting your relationship honestly.

And even more fundamentally, voicing your worries and concerns puts your old attachment style on the run. Because insecure attachment styles encourage us to subordinate our own worries and needs and to prioritize the concerns of others, by recognizing and then expressing your own concerns is the opposite of what an insecure attachment style wants you to do.

So, sharing worries with your partner not only exposes them to the cleansing power of daylight, but it also enlists your partner in your quest to put your old, insecure attachment style to rest once and for all.

Conclusion

I hope I've given you something to think about with this book. I further hope that I've given you hope–hope that you have the power within you to let go of the unhealthy patterns of your past and seize a happier, healthier, and more honest tomorrow.

Before I wrap things up, I'd like to say a word about my professional field: psychotherapy.

You might have noticed that I haven't mentioned psychotherapy as a vehicle for personal transformation.

As I stated at the outset, my intention with this book is not to replace therapy, but to introduce you to the ideas that are at the heart of the therapeutic process. I am certain that many of the people who read this book have the resources within themselves to make the journey beyond their insecure attachment styles on their own–or rather, with the help of their friends, family and loved ones (unless those people have an investment in your not changing–and that does happen.)

For those who find that the hill is too steep to climb on their own, and their deeply ingrained repetitive patterns too stubborn, psychotherapy is an invaluable tool to reaching the same destination. For these folks, I will say that there is absolutely nothing weak about seeking therapy. In fact, it's a sign of strength when you are able to admit that you need help in gaining the perspective you need to adjust your life's journey to a healthier, happier heading.

Thank you to all the readers of this book. I hope you have found it helpful, and I encourage you to seek out other resources that will help you round out your understanding of yourself and your place in the world.

Because the truth is you are important. The truth is this planet needs as many well-rounded, self-fulfilled and healthy people as it can get. You have a lot to offer–to yourself, to a partner, and to everyone else. Look within yourself, discover that which makes you special, then go out and share it with the world.

About The Author

Marc Sholes has been practicing psychoanalysis since 1986, with a focus on individuals and couples. He also writes, teaches, and supervises analysts-in-training. He lives in New York City with his wife and three children. He is still waiting for the green light from his wife for a dog.

Printed in Great Britain
by Amazon